WE ALL HAVE ~~PROBLEMS~~ SOLUTIONS

ROGER HERNÁNDEZ

Pacific Press® Publishing Association

Nampa, Idaho | Oshawa, Ontario, Canada
www.pacificpress.com

Cover design by Steve Lanto
Cover design resources from iStockphoto.com/Steve Debenport
Interior design by Kristin Hansen-Mellish

Copyright © 2018 by Pacific Press® Publishing Association
Printed in the United States of America
All rights reserved

The author assumes full responsibility for the accuracy of all facts and quotations as cited in this book.

Unless otherwise noted, all Scripture quotations are taken from the Holy Bible, New Living Translation, copyright © 1996, 2004, 2007, 2013, 2015 by Tyndale House Foundation. Used by permission of Tyndale House Publishers, Inc., Carol Stream, Illinois 60188. All rights reserved.

Scripture quotations marked CEV are from Contemporary English Version®. Copyright © 1995 American Bible Society. All rights reserved.

Scripture quotations marked GNT are from the Good News Translation® (Today's English Version, Second Edition). Copyright © 1992 American Bible Society. All rights reserved.

Scripture quotations marked NIV® are from THE HOLY BIBLE, NEW INTERNATIONAL VERSION®. Copyright © 1973, 1978, 1984, 2011 by Biblica, Inc.® Used by permission. All rights reserved worldwide.

Additional copies of this book are available for purchase by calling toll-free 1-800-765-6955, or by visiting http://www.adventistbookcenter.com.

Library of Congress Cataloging-in-Publication Data
Names: Hernandez, Roger, 1967- author.
Title: We all have problems / Roger Hernandez.
Description: Nampa : Pacific Press Publishing Association, 2018.
Identifiers: LCCN 2018027942 | ISBN 9780816364381 (pbk. : alk. paper)
Subjects: LCSH: Christian life—Textbooks. | Conflict management—Religious aspects—Christianity—Textbooks. | Problem solving—Religious aspects—Christianity—Textbooks.
Classification: LCC BV4511 .H47 2018 | DDC 248.8/6—dc23 LC record available at https://lccn.loc.gov/2018027942

July 2018

Dedication

This book is dedicated to Kathy. Falling in love with you was easy.
Staying in love is wonderful. You reflect in your own life
how God's grace can overcome any problem.

Contents

Introduction 7

Part 1—We All Have Problems
    Chapter 1: The Problem of Impatience 13
    Chapter 2: The Problem of Failure 21
    Chapter 3: The Problem of Finances, Part 1 .. 31
    Chapter 4: The Problem of Finances, Part 2 .. 41
    Chapter 5: The Problem of Pain and Suffering,
        Part 1 53
    Chapter 6: The Problem of Pain and Suffering,
        Part 2 61
    Chapter 7: The Problem of Family 69
    Chapter 8: The Problem of Disconnection ... 77

Part 2—We All Have Hope
    Lesson 1: Trouble 87
    Lesson 2: Connection 91
    Lesson 3: Priorities 95
    Lesson 4: Dollars and Sense 98
    Lesson 5: Hurt 103
    Lesson 6: Transformation 107
    Lesson 7: Failure 111
    Lesson 8: Rest 115
    Lesson 9: Life 119
    Lesson 10: Faith 123

Introduction

Moses is one of the best-known biblical characters. From the first time I read his story (as well as seeing it personified in the classic movie *The Ten Commandments*), I identified with his experiences. His life, just the same as mine (and possibly yours), was characterized by victories and defeats, feats and failures, obedience and sin. He wasn't from Egypt, yet through a series of miraculous events he came to know power, fame, riches, and royalty in Egypt. He had good moments and terrible tragedies. This book is a summary of the parallels between Moses, God, you, and me.

His story is found in the first books of the Bible. Movies tend to glamorize his life, but his experiences are relatable and beneficial. He struggled with insecurities, had a family he cared about, and made some mistakes along the way.

As you read this book, you will see me draw from Moses' experiences in order to glean helpful insight that will bless your life. I use a Bible passage at the beginning of each chapter and develop that concept though the ensuing chapter, supporting it with other Bible passages. This is called application.

We All Have ~~Problems~~ Solutions

When we apply the Bible to our lives, we start seeing the change that we crave.

Many people see Scripture as either irrelevant or as only for holy people. It is neither. Scripture was written with you in mind, with Jesus at its center. It is amazing that this ancient book can be so relevant today.

"The Bible was written over a 1,600-year period by approximately 40 men."[1] Numerous secular historians and archeologists confirm many parts of its narrative. It contains "more than 3,200 verses with fulfilled prophecy either within the Bible itself or since the Bible was written."[2]

In other words, it's just not another book. Don't take my word for it. Let's study it together, remembering that the primary purpose of the Bible is transformation, not information. Spiritual transformation, as with most life transformations (like losing weight), takes time.

If you look in the mirror and don't like what you see, you have options.

- You can concentrate on your current condition while screaming and regretting it to the point that you give up exercising.
- You can ignore it at your peril, continue living your present lifestyle, and throw away all the mirrors in your house.
- You can start an exercise routine, modify your diet, and get some sleep. You under-

Introduction

stand that this is for the long haul; you're looking for results in the long term and envisioning yourself achieving the desired objective.

Something similar happens on the spiritual plane. First, decide to allow God to transform you. Then, have patience with your progress, because the change will come. God has not finished His work in you.

---

1. "Facts that Support the Bible is the Inspired Word of God," Scientists For Jesus, accessed June 14, 2018, https://scientistsforjesus.wordpress.com/2013/11/16/facts-that-suppor-the-bible-is-the-inspired-word-of-god/.

2. "Facts that Support."

Part 1

We All Have Problems

Chapter 1

The Problem of Impatience

Many years later, when Moses had grown up, he went out to visit his own people, the Hebrews, and he saw how hard they were forced to work. During his visit, he saw an Egyptian beating one of his fellow Hebrews. After looking in all directions to make sure no one was watching, Moses killed the Egyptian and hid the body in the sand.

—Exodus 2:11, 12

I am not patient. Traffic jams make me very impatient. I always ask myself why the lane I'm driving in is usually the slowest. I get frustrated when people tell stories without getting to the point. I don't like to wait on the phone, listening to music. My initial impulse, like Moses in the verses above, is to act first, think later.

This attitude has caused me problems. God is helping me to change, but I need more help. Perhaps you identify with me on this. Could there be a way to change?

This dilemma presents itself particularly when my wife and I go out to eat. First of all, when the waiter comes, I already know what I want, and I am ready to order. Why waste time? My wife, with her analytical eye, asks for more time to analyze the menu. After finally ordering the food, I scarf it down right away. My wife looks at the food, evaluates it, enjoys it, savors it. I usually finish my food way before her, and then I do something that annoys her. I try her food.

The result? I have fork marks on my hands that remind me it is important to be patient. Here are principles of patience I want to share:

1. Impatience is a human problem.

Moses was leading his people from the slavery and servitude of Egypt to the Promised Land. But the way was long. Note the italicized words in the passage: "Then the people of Israel set out from Mount Hor, taking the road to the Red Sea to go around the land of Edom. *But the people grew impatient with the long journey.*" (Numbers 21:4; emphasis added).

Perhaps you feel like the Israelites. You never finish journeying to your destiny. One year ends, and the next begins, and you think, *This is my year.* However, you encounter more of the same. If you're honest, you even question whether God really exists or is interested in what happens to you. Situations such as these arise:

- A marriage that never gets better
- Children who get into trouble and don't learn
- Debts that never go away

- A diet that doesn't work

You live stuck in the middle—not where you were, but also not where you want to be. This produces impatience. *Until when, God? When will it be my turn? The journey is long, the desert inhospitable, and my patience is wearing thin.* What can you do? This brings us to the second principle.

2. The force behind your impatience is a desire for control.

The reason we become impatient is that human nature likes to be in control. It's a natural desire to want to know what will happen and how. Anxiety increases with uncertainty. We don't like verses such as, "Our God is in the heavens, and he does as he wishes" (Psalm 115:3).

I would like to tell you that, yes, you can predict what will happen and, if you work hard and you're honest, everything will go right for you. The reality is that there are no controlled results. No one—not even religious types who assure you that if you do A, B, and C, then D will happen—is always correct. A lot of the time, we are more comfortable with a God who simply endorses our decisions versus the God who orders our steps. One of the most difficult things to learn about life is how to let God control it.

I would like to be able to tell you that there are always predetermined results. I'd like to tell you that life is like my Father's Day gift. What do I mean?

Trying to exercise regularly, I began to look for resources to aid me. I saw this watch called a Fitbit that counts your steps, your heart rate, and your calories. I wanted one for Father's Day. Understand that Father's Day is not like Mother's Day. Mothers get breakfast in bed, fancy presents, and poems on Facebook. Fathers get toast and another necktie. So my probability of getting a Fitbit for Father's Day was between zero and nothing. I hatched a plan—guaranteed results.

I sat my family down and told them, "This coming Father's Day, I would like for you to get me a Fitbit. Here's one hundred and fifty dollars so you can buy it." What do you think happened? I got it! Unfortunately, there are few things in life that we can control to this degree.

When I feel the temptation to be impatient, I ask myself, "What part of this situation do I want to control?" I realize that behind my impatience is a real and intense desire for things to turn out the way I want them to. I invite you to have a chat with God the next time you feel impatient. Give your anxiety and worries to Him. It's going to be difficult, but it can be learned.

3. You can't speed up God's blessings, but you can certainly delay them.

Moses and his 1.6 million followers left slavery in Egypt and headed for the Promised Land. A trip

The Problem of Impatience

that should have taken days took decades. Why? The apostle Paul provides a clue: "And don't grumble as some of them did, and then were destroyed by the angel of death. These things happened to them as examples for us. They were written down to warn us who live at the end of the age" (1 Corinthians 10:10, 11).

The Israelites complained about everything. Going around the desert in circles was not God's idea, but was the consequence of a negative spirit that demonstrated they were not ready to arrive where God wanted to take them. Every time they complained, God looked from heaven and said, "Another lap around the desert!"

"We don't like the food You give us, Lord. Manna [a special bread God gave them daily] in the morning, afternoon, and night. We're tired of manna!"

"Oh, you don't like the food? Another lap!"

"We don't like this leader you put over us, Lord. He sticks to his family and doesn't do what we want."

"You don't like the leader? Okay. Another lap!"

"We don't like the water; it's bitter."

"Don't like the water? That's cool. Another lap!"

Maybe the same thing is happening to you. You are in a desert in your life, going around in circles without getting anywhere. There's movement, but no progress. There's action, but no success. It feels like a carousel: a lot of moving about, but in the end you find yourself in the same place you started out from—only now with the infernal carousel music stuck in your head.

Remember that you can't speed up your blessing. You can only delay it.

4. Do you want to be an oak or a mushroom?

The mushrooms that you can find in your garden sprout, grow, and die within a day. On the other hand, the oak in your yard grows much more slowly, but it can weather terrible storms. Success with Christianity—and, really, with all life in general—can be summarized in two words: Takes time.

Places worth going don't have shortcuts. When you are patient, God promises that He will work in your favor. Consider this verse: "For since the world began, no ear has heard and no eye has seen a God like you, who works for those who wait for him!" (Isaiah 64:4).

Remember that, with patience, even the snail was able to board Noah's ark.

5. The promise that is most difficult to wait for

You've probably heard that Jesus will return to this world to eliminate all evil and restore everything good. People have been waiting for His arrival for more than two thousand years. The Israelites waited 450 years for their promised liberation, which came through Moses. It is difficult to wait. At times, it's easy to become cynical and ask, as the Israelites did, "Until when, Lord?"

The Problem of Impatience

In the middle of this wait, allow me to share a bit of hope. Another biblical author, who was also a disciple of Jesus and saw Him ascend to heaven, tells us, "The Lord isn't really being slow about his promise, as some people think. No, he is being patient for your sake. He does not want anyone to be destroyed, but wants everyone to repent" (2 Peter 3:9).

Allow me to introduce you to a concept commonly called "hope." Hope is living with certainty and patience while what is promised is on its way. Imagine that two employees are asked to do the same job: install cabinet doors. The same work—doing the same thing day after day, week after week—can become tedious. Now imagine that one of these employees was told he would receive fifteen dollars as a bonus at the end of the year, and the other was told he would receive a fifteen-dollar bonus at the end of the job. Do you think there would be a difference in the way they did the same work? The former would probably begin to complain at some point, and the latter would be whistling while he worked. The difference between them is hope.

The reason you can hope for the coming of Jesus is that you can study the Bible and understand that what God promises, He fulfills. Paul reminds us of the connection between hope and patience: "Rejoice in our confident *hope*. Be patient in trouble, and keep on praying" (Romans 12:12; emphasis added). With hope, the heart becomes glad, even

We All Have ~~Problems~~ Solutions

though the current circumstances are not the best. Hope gives us patience, and prayer reminds us that we have hope. Hope reminds us that our worst day is not our last day. Live with hope. Live with patience.

"So let's not get tired of doing what is good. At just the right time we will reap a harvest of blessing if we don't give up" (Galatians 6:9).

Chapter 2

The Problem of Failure

> Good planning and hard work lead to prosperity,
> but hasty shortcuts lead to poverty.
>
> —Proverbs 21:5

Today Moses is seen as a tremendous leader. Many movies have been made about his life. Books have been written about his experiences. Sermons, videos, music. In reality, Moses, as you and I have, tasted failure. For every one of his feats, he experienced a corresponding failure. This started early in his life. Read these verses carefully:

> Many years later, when Moses had grown up, he went out to visit his own people, the Hebrews, and he saw how hard they were forced to work. During his visit, he saw an Egyptian beating one of his fellow Hebrews. After looking in all directions to make sure no one was watching, Moses killed the Egyptian and hid the body in the sand.
>
> The next day, when Moses went out to visit his people again, he saw two Hebrew

We All Have ~~Problems~~ Solutions

men fighting. "Why are you beating up your friend?" Moses said to the one who had started the fight.

The man replied, "Who appointed you to be our prince and judge? Are you going to kill me as you killed that Egyptian yesterday?"

Then Moses was afraid, thinking, "Everyone knows what I did." And sure enough, Pharaoh heard what had happened, and he tried to kill Moses. But Moses fled from Pharaoh and went to live in the land of Midian.

When Moses arrived in Midian, he sat down beside a well (Exodus 2:11–15).

Moses went to a desert far from everything he knew—for forty years. A wanted man with a past.

What do we do when we fail and feel forgotten? When failure touches us, the most important question we need to ask is why we have failed. Most of the time, we can find the answer. A good place to start is the Bible.

The Bible gives us six reasons for failure. The first reason for failure that the Bible gives is *disconnection from God*.

"The Lord himself will send on you curses, confusion, and frustration in everything you do, until at last you are completely destroyed for doing evil and abandoning me" (Deuteronomy 28:20).

Before continuing, I would like to emphasize a concept we should all have clear in our minds: our

The Problem of Failure

salvation comes only by grace through faith. We don't deserve it, we cannot earn it, and we have no merits through which to acquire it. Just as salvation obtained through grace brings blessings, obedience also brings blessings.

There are many biblical examples of the connection that exists between obedience and blessings. The Bible also shows the connection between disobedience and failure. Not everyone who disconnects from God fails immediately, but the majority of people who have experienced failure did so due to living disconnected from God at some point in their lives.

In fact, it could be that your life is not as marvelous as you would like it to be. Plan A, plan B, and plan C didn't work out. It could be that everything you touch turns into dust, not gold. "Crisis" is your middle name; problems and difficulties are your constant companions. If you are experiencing failure in this moment, I invite you to make examining your relationship with God your priority. The further you are from God, the closer you are to failure. The reason Moses failed was his tendency to depend on himself and not God. I'm not saying that paroximity to God eliminates all our problems, but His presence in our lives makes a positive difference.

Remember the following:

- Just because you don't feel His presence

does not mean that it is not real.
- Just because you don't see His work in you does not mean that He is not doing it.
- Just because you don't agree with His plan does not mean His plan is not correct.

The second reason people fail is *a tendency to attempt shortcuts.*

Seeing his people attacked, Moses made a rushed decision instead of looking for the advice and support of God. A shortcut is a method of finishing a task in the least amount of time possible. But there are things in life that don't need to be done quickly. Patience is not like fast food; it's like Thanksgiving dinner.

There is a direct connection between impatience and shortcuts. Taking shortcuts in life is the outward manifestation of an internal reality. Remember the biblical principle we learned to overcome impatience: You cannot accelerate God's blessings, but you can do all sorts of things that delay them.

The great truth is that the quickest way to delay a blessing is a bad attitude. The bad attitude makes us say the following things:

- Why did I marry him?
- Why doesn't God bless me?
- Why don't my kids act like everyone else's?
- Why did that person get a promotion and not me?

The Problem of Failure

- How come she got married and I'm still single? Lord, don't you see the way she is?

In twenty-five years of being a pastor, I have seen many people fail as a consequence of this second reason, taking shortcuts—which leads to bad attitudes—in areas of life such as the following:

- *Relationships*—Loneliness can really affect us. I understand that being single while we watch our friends get married is a difficult thing. But a rushed relationship can devastate our lives. Don't rush love.
- *Finances*—There simply is no legitimate strategy to get rich quick. Studies show that the vast majority of people who win the lottery spend or lose all the money soon afterward. Investing in pyramid schemes or not knowing anything about the investments they're making can destroy people financially and leave them penniless.
- *Jumping from one thing to another*—The temptation to quit whatever's not working out is real. Be careful about jumping ship because a situation seems external when, in reality, the problem is internal. It doesn't matter where we run, the problem will follow us. Only the power of God will sustain us; therefore, be patient.

We All Have ~~Problems~~ Solutions

The reason we take shortcuts and end up failing is that we continually reaffirm the idea that we know everything. The truth is that we really don't. We must allow God to take control. We will all encounter the following realities in life:

- There are things we will never be able to change. Therefore, we must leave them behind.
- There are things that change only slowly. Therefore, we must have patience.
- Of course, there are some things in life that need to change immediately. We must have the bravery to change them.

The solution is to have spiritual discernment to know which of the three is the correct thing for you to do.

The third reason people find themselves in the middle of failure is *pride*.

There is nothing wrong with having self-confidence. In fact, a person who believes in himself or herself should be sufficiently intelligent to recognize that they don't know everything, can't do everything, and need God's help to be successful. Accepting the errors they have made, and learning from those errors, is not a sign of weakness but of strength.

The life afforded Moses in the palace taught him to be prideful. That almost never ends well. The

The Problem of Failure

three most dangerous words in any language are "I already know." I have a teenage son who picked these words up quickly, probably from his mother (or, I don't know, maybe from me—who knows?). He loves to tell me how to arrange things, how to finish things, how to do any task—all the things an adult can do. I try to be patient with him because I remember being the same way at his age. But honestly, it's really hard. Pride brings us to failure in the following ways:

1. *Pride makes us difficult to relate to.* No one enjoys being around a know-it-all. I think know-it-alls don't even like being around themselves. The more intense a person's pride, the harder it is to relate to that person. The reason God had to relegate Moses to forty years of sheepherding in the desert was for Moses to learn that, before leading others, he had to learn to lead himself.

2. *Pride hurts others around us.* We act as if we are superior, which in turn denigrates others. We're incapable of admitting errors, which is frustrating for other people to deal with. We're not able to really hear people, which creates distance between them and us.

3. *Pride's roots are in the distorted vision we have of ourselves.* Those who have low self-esteem

may overcompensate by behaving pridefully. This serves only to distance the person from others, especially those the person loves. One of the things I always advise parents to do is to admit their faults to their children. Contrary to popular belief, admitting an error you committed against your child gives you more strength and earns your child's trust. Never admitting an error makes you weaker. The apostle Paul was correct when he wrote in Romans 12:16, "Live in harmony with each other. Don't be too proud to enjoy the company of ordinary people. And don't think you know it all!"

4. *It's hard to be blessed when you're busy being proud.* One of the quickest ways to delay or put an end to your best moments in life is to publicize all your triumphs with a loud, animated voice. The temptation to take God's glory and make it your own carries grave consequences. God does not share His glory with us. If God has begun to delay or block your triumphs, the first question you should ask yourself is, "Have I given the glory to God completely?" One of the most powerful verses that declares this truth to us is James 4:6, "And He gives grace generously. As the Scriptures say, 'God opposes the proud but gives grace to the humble.' "

The Problem of Failure

Many times I hear people blaming Satan for their own failures and lack of personal growth, when in reality it's God who is taking action in the situation in order to correct bad desires.

I'm a sports fanatic. My teams are the Cowboys, the Yankees, and any soccer team besides Argentina. One of the key questions any player asks himself is, "When is the right moment to retire?"

Many times we have seen excellent players who, because of pride, don't ask themselves that question. Because of their pride, they end up on the bench or "freed from" their contractual obligations to any team. It is very difficult for a player to admit that he can no longer play at the same level. There will always be someone younger, faster, better. The dark clouds of pride distort self-perception.

Because of this, it is important to surround ourselves with people who also tell us "you can't" rather than those who say "you can" even when they know you can't.

The Bible is very clear about pride. Pride precedes a fall and destruction (Proverbs 16:18). God knew that the Israelites were going to fail, and He created a place where they could go to confess their sins. It was called the sanctuary. The people went to the sanctuary to sacrifice innocent lambs, which symbolized God's desire to connect with His children and remind us that our failures are events—*they are not our identity*. Exodus 25:8 reveals the intense desire of a God who is always seeking to

We All Have ~~Problems~~ Solutions

relate to us, "Have the people of Israel build me a holy sanctuary so I can live among them."

How spectacular. God, being holy and perfect, wants to be with me, an imperfect sinner. Today we no longer sacrifice lambs, but we do go to the sanctuary (church) weekly to remember that God sent His only son to die for us. He is the Lamb of God who takes away the sin of the world.

When was the last time you went to church? There are people who only go three times in their entire lives. As the saying goes, the first time they throw water on you, the second time they throw rice, and the third time they throw soil. This is not the plan. We go to church weekly to worship the God who converts our failures into victory, to learn how to live in victory, and to help others so that they also can experience victory.

I invite you to come to church this Sabbath. If you want information about a church near you that worships, learns, and helps, you can find it on this page: https://www.adventist.org/en/utility/find-a-church. "May he send you help from his sanctuary and strengthen you from Jerusalem" (Psalm 20:2).

Chapter 3

The Problem of Finances, Part 1

So Moses returned to the Lord and said, "Oh, what a terrible sin these people have committed. They have made gods of gold for themselves."
—Exodus 32:31

There are two attitudes about money that are damaging.

One is that money doesn't matter. If you believe that, say so to the cashier the next time you go to pay for your food. Of course money matters.

The other attitude is that money is *all* that matters. This problem is the one Moses encountered in the verse above. Moses had a problem with the Israelites because, instead of using gold, they worshiped it.

These two problems continue today. There are people so negligent with their finances that they hurt their families through being constantly disorganized with it and lacking any financial progress. On the other hand, people also experience pain when all they care about is getting more, to the point that they neglect the people they love.

What is the key to having a healthy financial life? Where is the balance? How can we use money without worshiping it?

Not too long ago I read an article about lottery winners. You would think that these people who were poor one day and rich the next would be fully enjoying their new reality. In most cases, though, the opposite happened. With more money came more problems. All of a sudden, family members they never knew appeared out of the woodwork, demanding money. They started to have family disputes that caused some winners to end up divorced.

Because their spending habits followed the same line of logic as betting on the lottery and winning, the same way the money came, it went. Many winners had the same amount of money five years later that they'd had before winning, but now they had lost significant relationships as well.

Then what is the key? Stop waiting for an old uncle to die and leave you an inheritance, or to win the lottery. The key is to follow the principles God has established in His Word that convert money into a tool rather than an idol. Perhaps you'll be surprised to know the Bible mentions finances more than two thousand times. God knew how important it would be for us to understand the subject.

One of the biggest issues in our society is a collective inability to manage personal finances with the wisdom that God has allowed us to obtain. The

The Problem of Finances, Part 1

purpose of this chapter is to establish clear financial principles that can be a blessing in your life. To reach this reality, you should understand three things about finances:

- The part you play concerning finances
- The dangers money can cause
- The purposes of money

Come along with me to discover the key to true prosperity.

My part

The first thing that should be clear is that you are the administrator, not the owner, of the money you have. The sooner you understand this concept, the better it will be for you. Let me ask you a question: If you earn one thousand dollars, how many of those dollars belong to God?

Most people answer, "One hundred dollars," because they're thinking of tithe, but this answer is incorrect. Everything is God's. When we think that only a part belongs to God, we manage the rest as though it is ours. Doing that is precisely what is messing us up. The Bible says, "The silver is mine, and the gold is mine, says the Lord of Heaven's Armies" (Haggai 2:8).

Although God asks you to return only a fixed percentage to Him while you are to administer the rest, don't get it twisted—you should administer

We All Have ~~Problems~~ Solutions

the part that stays with you according to biblical principles. When we believe that returning tithe means we can do whatever we want with the rest, we bring problems on ourselves. Let's not think this way. Biblical principles cannot be applied to one money bucket and not the other, spending what's left after tithe as if we don't know what the Bible says about debts, dishonest earnings, and materialism. One of the best Bible verses on this topic of financial administration says, "But don't begin until you count the cost. For who would begin construction of a building without first calculating the cost to see if there is enough money to finish it?" (Luke 14:28).

This short verse contains four biblical principles that ensure we administer our finances better.

Set goals. The person alluded to in the previous passage had three goals. First, he wanted to construct. Second, he wanted to construct towers. Third, he wanted to construct one tower at a time. Do you want to be a good financial administrator? Then you also should establish clear goals that are specific and realistic. Why are goals important? It's simple: If you don't know where you're going, you're already there. Just as Moses purposed to arrive at the Promised Land despite the obstacles, so can you. Anyone who has ever accomplished something significant did so by first setting goals.

Think first. Before beginning to build, the man first took a seat. Sitting implies thinking things over.

The Problem of Finances, Part 1

He didn't make emotional, rushed, or thoughtless decisions. The same advice applies to us. If we make financial decisions calmly, there will be less suffering afterward. The first thing we want to establish is what we feel are necessary things, like a car or a cell phone—which, by the way, a large part of the rest of humanity consider luxuries. If you live in an industrialized country, you are in the top two percent of the wealthiest people on the planet. In this context of general prosperity, it would do you well to utilize the wisdom God has given you to discern the difference between the following things:

- What is essential, and what is a whim or craving?
- What is necessary, and what is desired?
- What is indispensable, and what is a luxury?

The key question is this: What are you willing to do without to reach your financial goals?

A few years ago, my wife and I experienced a reduction in salary. This led us to review all our monthly expenses to see where we could cut back. We realized that we were spending $250 a month on our internet, cable, and landline together. We got rid of the whole package. When my kids found out they weren't going to have cable TV for a while, they almost had heart attacks.

I am pleased to report that they survived. We

We All Have ~~Problems~~ Solutions

found other, more productive ways to pass the time, like reading a book or playing outside, and no one died. What we learned during this period of austerity is that it's possible to live without certain comforts. A wise person can discern between the things that are really important and those that we have simply because our society says it should be that way, or because everyone has them.

Budget your expenses. The verse says, "to see if there is enough." What a powerful phrase. The question here is not, "What's the monthly payment?" but, "How much does it cost?" A budget is you telling your money where to go instead of you asking yourself where it went. If you go to the hospital one day with strong bodily pains and the X-ray shows you need surgery, what do you do?

You'll probably hear an infinite stream of advice from your grandmother, your mother, or your friends that includes various treatments to try to heal yourself. Maybe you want to try some homeopathic remedy or alternative method. At the end of the day, though, you realize that if they don't operate on you, your pain will continue and probably become more severe.

In the same way, when your finances are examined under the X-ray of a budget, you would do well to make the necessary changes as quickly as possible to avoid headaches in your marriage and your stability. Meditate on this: "Wise people think before they act; fools don't—and even brag about

The Problem of Finances, Part 1

their foolishness" (Proverbs 13:16).

Always persevere. Many lives are full of projects initiated, but few projects are completed. Persevere, and you will discover the immense pleasure of seeing something finished. You cannot obtain prosperity in one day; it is obtained through making the correct decisions every day. Persevere until you are out of debt.

Getting out of debt is like losing and gaining weight. Which is easier? People who want to lose weight go out to run, wearing a plastic bag to sweat more, thinking it burns extra calories. They don't eat for a whole week, and when they weigh themselves, they take note of having lost a single pound.

They celebrate by going out to eat, have some rice and tortillas, fried plantains, and soda, followed by a serving of flan. They weigh themselves, and they've gained five pounds. (I'm exaggerating a little here, but you get the point.)

The same happens when we want to get out of debt. We need to persevere, we need to strive, and we need to have patience. It is possible with perseverance.

Moses and the Israelites are an excellent illustration of this principle. The desert in which they passed forty years was nothing easy—it had heat, snakes, lack of food, and undrinkable water; setting up tents, taking them down. But the people persevered until they arrived. No one ever said it would be easy, but returning to Egypt was not an option. Persevere, and you will see better days.

We All Have ~~Problems~~ Solutions

The dangers

There are two dangers we should avoid:

Don't allow yourself to be seduced. Biblical advice says: "But watch out, or you may be *seduced* by wealth" (Job 36:18; emphasis added). The key word to reflect on is "seduce." This word has more to do with the heart than the mind. It speaks to us of feelings, of passion, of interest. We often hear phrases like:

- I fell in love with the car, and I bought it.
- I fell in love with that dress.
- I fell in love with that house.

I ask myself, "How can an inanimate object cause a person to fall in love with it?" This danger is exactly the one God wants to help us avoid. Jesus said of this dilemma, "No one can serve two masters. For you will hate one and love the other; you will be devoted to one and despise the other. You cannot serve God and be enslaved to money" (Matthew 6:24).

Don't get obsessed. One who is in love with a person who cannot or will not return that love could fall into obsession. If you allow money to be the object of your love, it will be easier than you think to move from seduction to obsession. The reason is simple: Material things cannot love you back. There are only two options in how you treat money: either you control it or it controls you. You may think you

The Problem of Finances, Part 1

have it under control, but before you conclude that you do, answer these questions:

- Do you neglect your family because of work?
- Is it difficult for you to stop working when you're at the office?
- Do you think about work during your time off or vacations?
- What is the first thing you think about when you get up, or the last thing you think about before you go to bed?
- Do you think about work or your finances when you pray, read the Bible, or attend church?
- Do you buy things because they're on sale, even though you really don't need them?
- When you go out to eat, do you eat more if someone else is paying?
- Is having more money the objective of your life?

A woman received the news that her husband was standing on the ledge of the tenth floor of a building and wanted to commit suicide.

"My love!" she cried. "Don't kill yourself! You have so much to live for! You cannot die now! We have to pay the mortgage on the house, we have four years left to pay off the car, we just finished buying furniture on credit, and our kids are starting college this year! You can't leave us now!"

We All Have ~~Problems~~ Solutions

Sometimes our financial situation is so bad that it makes us want to jump from the tenth floor, or at least throw the bill collectors who call us at dinnertime from that height. Don't get desperate! With the help of God, we have hope. We can begin to change our situation bit by bit, day by day, dollar by dollar. Remember that gold is to be used, not worshiped.

And now we have arrived at the second part of this topic.

Chapter 4

The Problem of Finances, Part 2

So Moses returned to the Lord and said, "Oh, what a terrible sin these people have committed. They have made gods of gold for themselves."
—Exodus 32:31

In 1996 I found myself studying at Andrews University, living in Michigan with my wife and my oldest daughter, Vanesa. One day a friend shared with us an "incredible plan" that would bring us out of poverty. Very convinced of what he was saying, he animatedly invited us to a meeting where the details would be explained.

Curious, we attended the appointment. There they presented us with the tremendous plan to reach "financial independence"—the process by which to become rich, and as a result, happy. It would be really easy. We only had to do two things: sell long-distance calling cards, and find three people to contact three others, in that way continuing the sales chain.

If we did that (according to them, something very easy to do), we would receive a percentage of

We All Have ~~Problems~~ Solutions

the earnings from what the others sold. This would enable our family not to have to work anymore, and we would be able to stay home, just waiting for the paychecks to arrive. To drive his point home, the presenter showed everyone in attendance a check that he had already received for his sales. *How marvelous! How moving! How easy!*

Those of us who wanted to get in on the plan needed to contribute only $360 up front in order to enjoy this unique opportunity. The faster we joined this company, the more earnings we would have. To calm our minds, the presenter explained that if "for some reason" we were not able to sell a lot of those cards and did not want to continue with the business, we could return the product. At that time, the $360 we had invested would be returned to us.

With a guarantee like that, my wife and I decided to embark on such a safe enterprise, because our enthusiasm was ready to go and our desire to earn money was very great. (Can someone say golden calf?) The thought that many people would buy calling cards from us motivated us greatly, because we had a lot of friends to whom we could present the business. We were excited, and our expectations for success grew bigger and bigger.

But there was a problem. No one was buying long-distance calling cards. On top of it, we had forgotten one small detail: We lived in a very small town where the majority of our neighbors were students (better translated as "those who have no

The Problem of Finances, Part 2

money") like us. To be honest, neither my wife nor I really enjoy knocking on doors to sell something. That was a real problem.

Over the course of a couple weeks, we tried to contact various friends, but some were already selling cards themselves, and others just weren't interested. Finally, we accepted the sad truth: There's no such thing as easy money, and if something seems too good to be true, it probably is.

We remembered what had been said at the presentation: If we returned the cards, we could get our money back. So we decided to return the product and recuperate the investment. We called the company, and they told us to pack all the cards in a box and mail the cards back, which we did. We waited a week, two weeks, three. By the third week, we called the company again to find out why our money was not arriving and discovered the number was disconnected.

We ended up losing the $360, plus the $10 we had spent on postage, and worst of all, we did not even use a single one of those calling cards ourselves. One our friends did a little better; he never got his money back, but he was more than ready to use those lucky cards.

The purposes of money

Money is amoral, meaning it is neither good nor bad. It is like a brick, which can either be used to construct a beautiful chimney or to break your

We All Have ~~Problems~~ Solutions

neighbor's window when he has his music blasting at maximum volume at 3 A.M. Money is not the problem in and of itself; the problem is how it is used. Money adopts the characteristics of its owner, only growing what the owner already is. There are three reasons why God created money:

It should be saved. Experts say that, at the very least, we should save five percent of what we earn in each paycheck. The principle of saving is one that we will discuss later, but let's agree here that it is important to develop this habit. Why is it important?

- *Truly being wealthy is a matter of what you have, not what you owe.* In a world of appearances, not everything we see really is the way it looks. Owning a luxurious house, driving the newest car, and wearing the latest fashions are not necessarily a sign of wealth. On the contrary, they could be a sign of deep debt. Saving is having. Credit is owing.
- *Saving brings security and mental peace.* The sleep of a person with savings will never be like the sleep of someone who, as we commonly say, "doesn't even have anything to wear to his own funeral."
- *Saving allows us to face the unforeseen without needing to incur debt.* The sudden loss of employment, an accident, the death of a loved one, the depreciation of a car, or a

The Problem of Finances, Part 2

boiler breaking down in the middle of the winter—aside from the pain or stress that these things can cause, we're better able to handle them if we have money saved up.
- *Saving allows us to take advantage of opportunities when they present themselves.* Whether the set of pans or knives that the lady of the house wants is now on sale, or the dream vacation, or the car we want, or the house we want, perhaps the son's school trip, the sleek laptop half off—whatever the opportunity presented to us, if we have savings, we will find it much easier to seize.
- *Saving facilitates the future; by having debt, we abuse it.* By incurring debt, we use our future as collateral for the things we are acquiring in the present. When we save, we prepare ourselves for a life of greater prosperity—one in which we have control.
- *Saving is a method of guaranteeing familial stability.* Wherever there are lawsuits and problems or angers and disappointments amongst family, it usually has to do with a lack of financial resources and/or misusing money. When you have the discipline to save, things are very different.
- *Saving gives our children better opportunities.* The more we go to great lengths to facilitate and equip them in their careers,

the more successful they will be. Saving to guarantee they can get an education is an investment that will pay great dividends in satisfaction and fulfillment.
- *Saving enables us to give more to God's work and to those in need.* When we're saving rather than living a lifestyle of indebtedness, we will have the blessing of being able to give to God and the needy without remorse or delay.

Meditate on what the Bible says: "Wise people think before they act; fools don't—and even brag about their foolishness" (Proverbs 13:16).

Part of saving is working from a good budget, as we mentioned in the previous chapter. Here is a very practical exercise that can surely help you organize your family budget. For two months, ask for and save the receipts for every single thing you buy or bill you pay, even if it is as minute as a can of soda or as big as the mortgage payment. When the two months end, you will discover the following:

- *We spend the most money on little things.* The mortgage and the car payment are not what left you with no money; it was all the eating out and little snacks here and there.
- *We need discipline to follow a good budget.* It's hard to say no to spending an amount that seems negligible on something we

The Problem of Finances, Part 2

consider small. That's why both people involved, the man and the woman, need to be in agreement ahead of time about how they will spend their money and how much to spend.

Below you'll find an example of a simple budget. Modify it, change it, minimize it, but please, put it into practice.

Priority	Category	Percentage of Salary
1	God (tithe and offering)	Tithe: 10
		Offering: 1–5
2	Rent/mortgage	20–35
3	Food	15–25
4	Transportation	10–15
5	Clothing	5
6	Medical	5
7	Savings	5–10
8	Entertainment/recreation	3–5
9	Debts	0–10
10	Unexpected expenses	3–5

It should be given away. When we give, we add value to others, and we make God smile. A philanthropist once said, "I use a shovel to dig out the money I give God, and He does the same in return. The interesting part is God's shovel is much bigger than mine."

When we give to God first, we are making a

spiritual declaration that we are givers first and consumers second. This is the *open hand* principle. This principle is simple, but very important. When we extend our open hands to God, He fills them, but He asks us not to close them so that others can benefit as well.

This principle is based in what we call the "firstfruits." The Bible tells us, "Honor the LORD with your wealth and with the best part of everything you produce" (Proverbs 3:9). This principle teaches us that the Lord does not ask *only* for ten percent, but for the *first* ten percent. When you give Him the first ten percent, you proclaim that you are a giver first and a consumer second. Your act of giving activates a blessing over the rest of the money that stays with you. Tithe is a minority percentage, a starting point, not an ending point. It is a basic way that we can acknowledge the sovereignty of God over all things, especially our finances.

There are some biblical cases regarding this firstfruits principle. They teach us that when we give God the first ten percent, it makes a big difference. I'll cite various cases and include a summary point for each so that you can study them later in more detail.

- Cain and Abel (Genesis 4:1–5): Note God's reaction to Abel, who brought the firstborn of his flock, while Cain brought whatever he had.

The Problem of Finances, Part 2

- Jericho (Joshua 6): God ordered that no one touch this city, which was the first city in Canaan that the Israelites conquered. Disobeying this explicit order had grave consequences.
- The Israelites (Deuteronomy 26): When the crops were harvested, the first of the harvest was for God. Not the tenth portion, but the first tenth. Moses taught the Israelites this principle.

These are only a few biblical examples. There are people who say, "Pastor, that was in the Old Testament. We're now living in the time of grace." I would respond to that rationale in this way: Although we are living under the dispensation of God's grace and we are not saved by the law, this New Testament reality ought to make us more faithful, not less. Grace doesn't lower the standard; it raises the standard.

For example, when Jesus spoke of adultery, He didn't lower the bar, He raised it (see Matthew 5:27–29). Grace doesn't cause us to give less, but makes us ask ourselves, "How can I give *more* to Someone who loved me so much He was willing to die for me?" This biblical teaching is not optional.

Some recommend that if you are unable to give firstfruits, the first 10 percent, then you can start out by giving 5 percent and increasing the percentage little by little. This is akin to someone saying,

We All Have ~~Problems~~ Solutions

"Last year I robbed ten banks; this year, by the grace of God, I want to improve. I will rob only five." Partial obedience is total disobedience.

It should be enjoyed. The following biblical passage establishes this principle clearly: "And it is a good thing to receive wealth from God and the good health to enjoy it. To enjoy your work and accept your lot in life—this is indeed a gift from God" (Ecclesiastes 5:19). There are people who go years without taking a vacation, who work full time, part time, overtime, and all the time.

My question is—For what? We should avoid extremes. We should not be inveterate spenders. Rather, we should spend prudently, and from time to time spend on activities and things we can enjoy, especially if we have a family. When the famous magnate John D. Rockefeller died, they asked his accountant, "How much did John leave behind?" The accountant responded, "Everything."

I invite you to visit a dumpster. There you will see electronics, clothing, wood from a house—basically thousands of things that at one time had value. Many of those things rotting away today are left over from marriages that ended, friends who became enemies, values that were compromised, families that were neglected, objects that grew old and wore out.

Let me ask you something. For what reason do you want to be prosperous? What do you

The Problem of Finances, Part 2

need money to do? How would you finish this phrase? "You will be enriched in every way so that _____" (2 Corinthians 9:11).

Some would answer the following:

- So that I can live well
- So that I can pay my bills
- So that I can provide for my family
- So that I can pay off the house
- So that I can have economic security

If God in His infinite mercy sent you a check for $1 million tomorrow, what would you do with it? In what way would you impact the world? How would you help your community?

God has a master plan for your life that includes using your resources, your wisdom, and your abilities to bless others. One of the verses that best reflects this reality can be found in what God says to Moses in Deuteronomy 28:13: "If you listen to these commands of the Lord your God that I am giving you today and if you carefully obey them, the Lord will make you the head and not the tail, and you will always be on top and never at the bottom."

Moses, the same as all the children of God, was blessed in order to be a blessing. I encourage you to draw up a plan with which you are going to help your community from today onward. Think big; dream further than what you can see in this moment, and prepare to put in practice what it is you

We All Have ~~Problems~~ Solutions

want when the opportunity comes. But start by doing something small today. Second Corinthians 9:11 from a few paragraphs ago ends this way: "You will be enriched in every way so that you can be generous on every occasion, and through us your generosity will result in thanksgiving to God" (NIV).

Chapter 5

The Problem of Pain and Suffering, Part 1

> Then Moses went back to the Lord and protested, "Why have you brought all this trouble on your own people, Lord? Why did you send me? Ever since I came to Pharaoh as your spokesman, he has been even more brutal to your people. And you have done nothing to rescue them!"
>
> —Exodus 5:22, 23

Moses had a dilemma. The people he loved were encountering a huge problem. He had left Egypt with the desire to liberate this people, but instead of liberation, they experienced more suffering.

The Israelites' reaction is understandable. When we suffer, we usually seek to know why and place blame instead of finding solutions.

They also were following a guide who was very human. For forty years, it was the same thing: As they walked through the desert on their way to the Promised Land, they encountered one problem after another that caused them pain. Sometimes it was a lack of water; sometimes it was eating the same food all day, every day; sometimes it was Moses' leadership style; sometimes it was the

We All Have ~~Problems~~ Solutions

danger of losing their lives to their enemies. They complained, got angry, and worried. God masterfully solved their problems and reprimanded their attitude. Yet, so quickly, they got spiritual amnesia, and the entire process would start over again. This vicious cycle repeated for forty years.

When I examine my life, I see the same patterns. I suffer from spiritual amnesia because I easily forget what God has done for me in the past, and I concentrate on the problems that I have in this moment. What does the Bible teach about the problem of pain and suffering? A lot.

One of my daughter's school friends died in a traffic accident. Gustavo was only seventeen years old when he died. He was a tremendous athlete and musician, came from a beautiful family, loved Jesus, and was a good example in his community. He had plans to go to university, get married, and audition for *American Idol*. That was his plan, but tragedy arrived before his dreams could become reality.

One of the last times I saw him was at a Bible study about how we can know God's will for our lives. He arrived on his motorcycle a little late, but happy. His personality and the things he said made the night memorable. Gustavo had a smile that would light up any room and a very positive perspective on life.

I was eating with my daughter on a Wednesday night after we'd hung out together, when one of Gustavo's best friends sent her a text message. It

The Problem of Pain and Suffering, Part 1

was only two words: "Gus died."

What had been a beautiful experience between father and daughter that day completely changed in an instant with just two words. That's how life is. Overnight, in an instant, plans change, and your world falls apart. The doctor gives you bad news about your tumor. You arrive home to find your spouse being unfaithful. You get a call from the police saying your son has been arrested.

When bad things happen to us, we can become depressed, despondent, and even desire to leave this world of pain behind. In the verses at the beginning of this chapter, we saw Moses angered by the danger that was coming ever closer to the Israelites. When we have problems and suffering, we usually prefer the dysfunction we're familiar with over the sanity that isn't familiar.

Perhaps you're feeling this way right now. Maybe you are going through moments of pain and suffering that have left you despondent. I want to share three principles that can help you come out of this experience stronger than you were before:

God has a plan, even if you don't understand it

When people are suffering, one of the things they always ask is, "Why?" It is a question that consumes us, one we return to over and over without necessarily finding an answer.

A while ago I was meditating on the "why" of a certain situation. God gifted me this phrase,

We All Have ~~Problems~~ Solutions

which I now share with you: "Do you want answers, or solutions?"

The answers to our questions can be understood only from the perspective of eternity, and we will fully understand the "why" only when we are in heaven. Until then, we should grab hold of the promises of God here, where we are now. God is not obligated to give us answers. What He has done is provide the solution. He has already conquered death. He has already conquered the grave. The worst problem that can happen to us on this earth, God has already solved. It is possible that you don't feel that way in this moment, but if you have patience and faith, you will see this truth for what it is.

Note what the apostle Paul says in 1 Corinthians 15:51, 52: "But let me reveal to you a wonderful secret. We will not all die, but we will all be transformed! It will happen in a moment, in the blink of an eye, when the last trumpet is blown. For when the trumpet sounds, those who have died will be raised to live forever. And we who are living will also be transformed."

There is hope even in death. The popular belief is that a person who dies goes to heaven if they were a good person and to hell if they weren't. This popular belief does not demonstrate the love of God. Take my case, for example. If I die today and go straight to heaven, how will I enjoy it, looking down and seeing my family suffering and crying?

The Problem of Pain and Suffering, Part 1

How would it make me happy to watch some other man marry my beautiful wife (even though she tells me she won't get remarried if I die before she does)?

What kind of God burns people for eternity? That God looks a lot like the devil. That God is not the God of the Bible. God does not burn people for eternity for these three reasons:

1. God only promises eternal life to those who believe in him (John 3:16). Think about it: If people are burning forever, that means they have eternal life—just not in heaven.
2. Burning forever is a punishment disproportionate to the crime. Saying that God will burn people for eternity for the things they did during a mere eighty years of life is contrary to common sense and contrary to the Master's character of love.
3. When the Bible speaks of eternal fire, it is referring to the duration of the *consequences* (results) of the fire, not to the duration of the burning itself.

Many people, especially young people, have rejected God because of this false teaching. A God who burns people for all eternity looks a lot like the devil, not the God of love whom we meet in the Bible.

God has a plan, even in the middle of your pain

God did not kill Gustavo in order to convert others. Death is a result of sin. We should put the blame on the one who deserves it: Satan. Good can come from sad experiences, however. Joseph said in Genesis 50:20, "You intended to harm me, but God intended it all for good. He brought me to this position so I could save the lives of many people."

I have seen myriad examples of this reality. The impact of Gustavo's life has been felt near and far. Various young people changed their lives. I believe Gustavo will have a few conversations in heaven with people he never met on earth. I'm sure one will tell him, "Gus, after you died, God changed my life. Thank you for the testimony you gave through the way you lived."

The worst that Satan can cause to happen to you is, in every case, something that God can use for your good. Probably more than one person reading these words has allowed the absence of prosperity to demotivate them. Let me give you advice—lift your head up. For a moment, look away from what is happening here and now, and concentrate on the blessing God is going to bring to your life and the lives of many others.

On a personal note, I give God thanks for everything He has given me. I also give Him thanks for everything He *hasn't* given me, even though I asked for it. Sometimes the most important prayers in our lives are the ones God answers differently than

The Problem of Pain and Suffering, Part 1

we think He should. When God allows something painful in your life, remember that He has a plan, even in the middle of the pain.

God has a plan, even if you do not agree with it

As a father and a human being, I reject death. I wish I could go back and change every moment that led Gustavo to where he is now. I understand on an intellectual level that God did not cause Gustavo's death, but on an affective and human level, it's impossible not to identify with his parents. Gustavo could have been one of my kids. He could have been one of yours. I am not always in agreement with what happens to me, but I have hope in the One who is within me.

The key is having faith even though _____ happens. Death happens. Separation from loved ones happens. Divorce happens. Cancer happens. Losing your job happens. Very rarely are you able to control what happens to you, but you can decide how you react. Instead of running far away from God when there's pain, you run to Him. He is big enough to hold all your tears, pain, and anger. You don't have to suffer alone. Nothing can separate you from His love.

This passage especially can bring you hope: "Can anything ever separate us from Christ's love? Does it mean he no longer loves us if we have trouble or calamity, or are persecuted, or hungry, or destitute, or in danger, or threatened with death? (As the Scriptures say, 'For your sake we are killed every day; we are being slaughtered like sheep.') No, despite all these things, overwhelming victory is ours through Christ, who loved us" (Romans 8:35–37).

I know that my daughter and I will see Gustavo again someday. Until then, I will believe in God's plan for my life, even if I don't understand or approve of it, or if it hurts. *Goodbye, despondency. Hello, Jesus.* "I am suffering and in pain. Rescue me, O God, by your saving power" (Psalm 69:29).

Chapter 6

The Problem of Pain and Suffering, Part 2

Then Moses went back to the Lord and protested, "Why have you brought all this trouble on your own people, Lord? Why did you send me? Ever since I came to Pharaoh as your spokesman, he has been even more brutal to your people. And you have done nothing to rescue them!"

—Exodus 5:22, 23

I hurt with the hurt of my people. I mourn and am overcome with grief. Is there no medicine in Gilead? Is there no physician there? Why is there no healing for the wounds of my people?

—Jeremiah 8:21, 22

We've all experienced hurts. For some, emotional and physical injuries are a constant reminder that words and actions matter. This theme is prevalent in the Scriptures. One of the ways human beings manage their emotions when they encounter pain looks a lot like the expression of Moses when he had an honest conversation with God. The whole of Moses's complaints can be reduced to two statements:

"Lord, why me?"

"Lord, You haven't done anything."

We All Have ~~Problems~~ Solutions

There are many causes of pain. Every time we experience pain, we say, "Why me? Why haven't You acted, God?" This chapter is practical. I want to give advice on how to face pain and suffering when they come knocking on your door—advice that helped Moses in the desert thousands of years ago and can help us today.

To get the most out of this chapter, you'll need something to write with. I invite you to do the exercises scattered throughout the chapter; they will help you.

Causes of pain

There exist at least four reasons for pain and suffering. Let's do an exercise together. Take a moment to internalize these categories and analyze them according to your life experiences. Assign a percentage to each one in terms of the quantity of pain experienced.

- Pain people have intentionally caused me: _____
- Pain people have unintentionally caused me: _____
- Pain I have intentionally caused myself: _____
- Pain I have unintentionally caused myself: _____

Pain can cause deep wounds, especially when

The Problem of Pain and Suffering, Part 2

you have not spoken of the wounds and have not forgiven those that caused them. Pain and suffering flourish in secrecy.

There are two important actions we need to take:

1. *Manage pain correctly.* According to recent studies, more than half of women have experienced some form of abuse, and even forty percent of men have as well. What can we do about this? Some lock the pain up inside; others ignore it or try to mitigate it with addictions. Instead of dwelling on abuse, seek out healthiness in God. He can bring emotional and physical health to your life.

   Most of us have suffered abuse or abandonment in four areas: physical, sexual, spiritual, or emotional. The negative effect of any one of these forms of abuse can destroy your relationship with God and with others. It is important to do two things: identify and forgive.

   Identify those who have hurt you, and forgive them. Perhaps you feel like the biblical writer who said in Job 30:9–11, "And now they mock me with vulgar songs! They taunt me! They despise me and won't come near me, except to spit in my face. For God has cut my bowstring. He has humbled me, so they have thrown off all restraint." Health doesn't come

We All Have ~~Problems~~ Solutions

immediately, but it is possible.

Please realize that healing from deep emotional wounds usually requires the help of mental health professionals. God can use human instruments to help soothe our pain.

2. *Forgive completely.* Resentment must be forsaken. It's like drinking poison yourself, and then standing there waiting for the rat to drop dead. By whatever means, we must forgive. This doesn't necessarily mean that the relationship is restored, or that you welcome an abuser back into your home. It means that you can treat people who have hurt you with respect and love. If you have been victimized, one crucial step toward healing is forgiveness. Who do you need to forgive today? Right now, today, pray for God to help you manage your pain, forgive, and grow afterward. If you have never experienced the pain of abuse, thank God for your blessings and help others to grow as human beings and release their pain and get out of it.

I don't mean to say this is simple. In many cases, it is exteremely difficult and may require a lengthier process.

The Cross of Christ taught us that the God of the Bible understands our pain, and that He is on our side to restore all things. While other religious

The Problem of Pain and Suffering, Part 2

philosophers teach humankind to begin working hard and exerting effort to reach God, Christianity teaches an all-powerful God who saved us by descending to earth and suffering our pains, providing a solution to the pain problem. Believe in Him. He understands. He heals.

Someone once said, "Peace is not the absence of problems, but the presence of God in the middle of them." Let's make today the day we analyze and understand how to react and move forward when problems come close to our lives and our families. The great reality of problems and blessings is that both come unannounced. Let's find the solutions together.

If you're experiencing problems, apply the following three principles:

Talk with God about the problem. The Bible tells us, "I pour out my complaints before him and tell him all my troubles" (Psalm 142:2). You do not have to carry your burdens alone. You don't need to feel like you're fighting on your own. What problem is affecting your life at the moment?

Stop worrying about the problem. Another beautiful verse reminds us, "So don't worry about tomorrow, for tomorrow will bring its own worries. Today's trouble is enough for today" (Matthew 6:34). Why is this a beautiful verse? Let me give you three reasons:

We All Have ~~Problems~~ Solutions

- Worrying makes no sense. If you can fix it, do so. If you can't, worrying will make no difference.
- Worrying will not improve anything; in fact, worrying makes problems bigger.
- Worrying does not increase your faith. When you worry, you minimize the power of God and increase your level of anxiety.

Believe in the help God provides to overcome problems. God directly shows us three methods to manage our problems appropriately:

- He frees us *from* the problem. "'Lord, help!' they cried in their trouble, and he rescued them from their distress" (Psalm 107:6).
- He gives us comfort *in* the problem. "He comforts us in all our troubles so that we can comfort others. When they are troubled, we will be able to give them the same comfort God has given us" (2 Corinthians 1:4).
- He will eventually eliminate *all* problems. "And God will provide rest for you who are being persecuted and also for us when the Lord Jesus appears from heaven. He will come with his mighty angels" (2 Thessalonians 1:7).

The good news is that God is bigger than any

The Problem of Pain and Suffering, Part 2

problem, He cares about me, and He is on my side.

Yet Jerusalem says, "The LORD has deserted us;
 the Lord has forgotten us."

"Never! Can a mother forget her nursing child?
 Can she feel no love for the child she has borne?
But even if that were possible,
 I would not forget you!" (Isaiah 49:14, 15).

How does it feel to know that your God will never abandon you? Take a moment to close your eyes right now and thank God that not only will He never leave you, He will never do anything to hurt you either. Allow His love to inundate your being. You are valuable to God.

I encourage you to do another exercise. With a red pen, or a pen of some other color, write the word "forgiven" over the names of the list that you made of people who have abused or abandoned you. Before reading each name, say this prayer: "My Father God, through Your grace and with Your power, I forgive _____. In the name of Jesus, amen."

The moment we forgive these people who did us wrong, we take away their power to continue hurting us. Not forgiving extends the pain; it does not reduce it. If we truly want to be healed, we must forgive. This is impossible for us, but God can do it. Therefore, we should connect ourselves with God, tell Him how impossible it is for us to forgive, and tell Him how much we need Him to help us. He will. "I tell you the truth, unless a kernel of wheat is planted in the soil and dies, it remains alone. But its death will produce many new kernels—a plentiful harvest of new lives" (John 12:24).

Chapter 7

The Problem of Family

> While they were at Hazeroth, Miriam and Aaron criticized Moses because he had married a Cushite woman. They said, "Has the Lord spoken only through Moses? Hasn't He spoken through us, too?" But the Lord heard them. (Now Moses was very humble—more humble than any other person on earth.)
>
> —Numbers 12:1–3

However lovely your family is, it will experience problems. The previous verses speak to us of one such occasion. The siblings of Moses—Miriam and Aaron—had a problem with the person Moses had chosen to be his permanent companion. She was dark-skinned and not their ideal. They simply didn't want her as a sister-in-law, so they criticized her. As if Moses didn't have enough problems already, he also had to watch his back because of his own siblings.

The word in the original language of the Bible translated as "humble" could also be interpreted as *depressed*. No surprise there. There are few things more painful than the people who you love the most hurting you in this way. This chapter is going

We All Have ~~Problems~~ Solutions

to explore various biblical passages that have to do with family. Whether you're married or single, there's something for you in this chapter.

Married people

"Live in harmony with each other. Don't be too proud to enjoy the company of ordinary people. And don't think you know it all!" (Romans 12:16).

Paul—who wrote at least thirteen books of the Bible, including the verse above—gives the key to having a happy family. Acknowledging that we don't know everything implies respecting the rights and individuality of the other persons in the family. Human beings are all different in three key areas:

- *How we look at life.* We're divided into groups of people who are systematic and people who are spontaneous. Systematic people love systems, plans, calendars. They frequently ask, "What's the plan?" On the other hand, spontaneous people live life singing the old hymn "One Day at a Time." They are much more focused on the present than the future.
- *How we relate to others.* There are two categories here as well: introverts and extroverts. If you think about emotions as a tank of gas, introverts use up gas to be around other people; extroverts fill up on being around people. The more people, the better

The Problem of Family

for extroverts. They're the first ones to get to the party and the last ones to leave. For an introvert, the situation is different. They prefer to be around family, and the fewer people, the more beautiful it is.
- *How we make decisions.* Some make decisions based on facts. "How much does it cost?" is the first question, not, "How does it feel?" Others make their decisions based on feelings. This difference especially affects couples when it comes to how they discipline their children.

If I could summarize the best three teachings for a happy marriage, I would tell you the following:

- Your partner is your complement, not your carbon copy. The person is different from you, and this doesn't make the person good or bad—just different!
- Women are not property. Men are not projects. It took me fifteen years to fully understand this fact, and when I did, it revolutionized my perspective.
- With God, marriage is hard; without God, it is impossible. Marriage is work. It has a lot of moments of happiness and deep connection, but that doesn't happen by chance. That's why you need the one who invented marriage—God.

We All Have ~~Problems~~ Solutions

Dating

If you are not yet married, here are seven quick bits of advice that can help you out. Choosing well is one of the determinant decisions in your life.

1. The person you choose should not have uncontrollable anger. "Don't befriend angry people or associate with hot-tempered people" (Proverbs 22:24). Uncontrollable anger reveals deep-seated insecurity and low self-esteem.
2. The person you choose should not have addictions. "Do not carouse with drunkards or feast with gluttons" (Proverbs 23:20). The reason to avoid someone who has any kind of addiction is that you will never come first, the addiction will.
3. The person you choose should not nurse resentment. People reflect what they resent. Hebrews 12:15 calls resentment the "root of bitterness." Holding on to resentment is like drinking poison and waiting for the rat to die.
4. The person you choose should not be selfish. Proverbs 28:25 tells us, "Greed causes fighting." If you marry a selfish man or woman, that person will never be satisfied with what they have.
5. The person you choose should not covet. Proverbs 15:27 reads, "Greed brings grief

The Problem of Family

to the whole family." If you marry someone who covets, you will be in debt your whole life.

6. The person you choose should tell the truth. "Truthful words stand the test of time, but lies are soon exposed" (Proverbs 12:19). Love's foundation is trust. If this person doesn't tell you the truth, you cannot trust them. If you can't trust this person, how can you love them?
7. The person you choose should put Jesus first. "Jesus replied, 'You must love the LORD your God with all your heart, all your soul, and all your mind' " (Matthew 22:37). I love this Jim Elliot quote: "God always gives His best to those who leave the choice with Him."

Turbulence

Some of you reading this book are asking yourselves what you're going to do, having so many problems it seems as if they will drown you. I know that sometimes marriage is hard and that there are times when you want to throw in the towel and run. Allow me to tell you a story about something that happened to my wife and me.

We had to travel from Michigan to Maryland, with a stop in Ohio, where there is a great lake that produces ferocious winds during the fall. It was November, and our first flight departed and landed without any mishaps. The problem began when we boarded the second airplane. Immediately we noticed that this "little airplane" was different. It only had sixteen seats total, in two rows of eight. My seat was in front of my wife's, and from where I sat, I could clearly see the pilot and all the controls in the cockpit.

After hearing the customary instructions, we took off. But the little plane began to move, shake, and wobble like paper carried away by the wind. My heart was beating a thousand times a minute. Internally, I confessed all my sins, known and unknown. My wife squeezed my hand so tightly that she stopped my blood circulation. It could have been my imagination, but to this day, I am almost certain I saw the pilot pull out a file marked "Only for Emergencies."

No one was reading a book or even speaking; we almost weren't breathing. It felt like a never-ending nightmare, until at last we were above the clouds, and the turbulence petered out. We stayed that way for a long while, but when the descent began, the apparent calm disappeared. Silence fell again, the discomfort returned, and I almost had three fingers broken. By God's grace, we landed, and we thanked Him for traveling mercies, but the only thing on my mind was the idea of strangling my travel agent.

What does this story about airplanes and hands squeezed like oranges have to do with marriage? A lot. That day I learned three lessons:

The Problem of Family

1. *Every marriage will have its turbulence.* Happiness is not guaranteed. When we get married, we embark on a long journey in which we will go through uncomfortable places. Sometimes there's only silence; in other moments, your hand gets squeezed to a pulp. The married life is similar to a plane trip. We can expect ups and downs at any moment.
2. *However difficult the situation, it's worse outside.* While Kathy and I were in the midst of the turbulence, it felt as serious as a heart attack. However, not a single passenger got up from their seat to say, "This is really bad. I'm getting out of here." Why not? Clearly, we were not comfortable inside the plane, but outside was worse. Many times the same happens in families. Uncountable people abandon their homes when they find themselves in the middle of conflict, believing the solution to their problems is a change of spouse. But how sad their condition when they realize they didn't solve anything. Plane trips without turbulence, and marriages without fights, only exist in the fantasy of Hollywood.
3. *The pilot knows what he is doing. He has flown that route before.* I'm not a pilot, I don't know anything about the state of Ohio, and I had never flown that route before. But my pilot had. When we board a plane, we are putting

our lives in the pilot's hands. We should do the same with our marriages. Jesus knows what He is doing, because He is the Pilot. Remember, He did not unite you in marriage to set you up for failure!

I'd like to make a special invitation. Would you like to give yourself and your family to the Lord Jesus Christ? Would you like it if we asked Him together? "The jailer called for lights and ran to the dungeon and fell down trembling before Paul and Silas. Then he brought them out and asked, 'Sirs, what must I do to be saved?' They replied, 'Believe in the Lord Jesus and you will be saved, along with everyone in your household.' And they shared the word of the Lord with him and with all who lived in his household" (Acts 16:29–32).

Chapter 8

The Problem of Disconnection

> The LORD said to Moses, . . . "Have the people of Israel build me a holy sanctuary so I can live among them. You must build this Tabernacle and its furnishings exactly according to the pattern I will show you."
>
> —Exodus 25:1–9

When I was a boy, I went to church a lot. I was there all day on Saturday, and every Sunday night, Monday night, Wednesday night, and Friday night. I wasn't born in the church (that would have been weird), but they did bring me there pretty much the next day.

In recent years, it has become more popular to say, "I believe in God, but I don't want anything to do with church." There's a movement, especially among young people, to see the church as something antiquated, obsolete, and disconnected from reality. If I'm perfectly honest, many times the people who say they are allergic to *ecclesia* are well-intentioned Christians who, whether due to zeal or dysfunction, have painted an image of God that is not real or biblical.

The verses above find our friend Moses being

instructed by God about a sanctuary. There are two important principles in these verses. Remember that although the instructions were given for a specific time and place, the principles behind them are eternal. Let's read the verses again:

"The Lord said to Moses, . . . 'Have the people of Israel build me a holy sanctuary so I can live among them. You must build this Tabernacle and its furnishings exactly according to the pattern I will show you' " (Exodus 25:1–9).

Encountering God was the primary purpose of the sanctuary. The exact instructions for the sanctuary and the services held within it depended on what God said, not on human ideas.

When the church functions well, it has these two characteristics. It is more than mere religious formality based on rites and traditions. It is an encounter with the Omnipotent One. It is based on precepts and divine directions, not human opinions or preferences. If we could truly understand the blessing it is to be able to go to church, many more would take the privilege seriously.

Let me share with you five reasons I gave the church another chance, and why you should consider doing the same.

1. *Friends for life.* I was at a church when I was hurt. That's a fact. But it's also a fact that at church I found friends who are still friends today. Friends who would give me one of

The Problem of Disconnection

their kidneys. Friends who risked their job so that I could keep mine. Friends who listen to me. Friends who love me. Friends who support me. Someone said that you cannot learn to swim without risking drowning. Human relationships with others are really difficult, but when you find a good friend, it's worth taking the risk of loving.

2. *Health.* In a study published in *The New York Times*, researchers found that going to church "boosts the immune system and decreases blood pressure. It may add as much as two to three years to your life."[1] People who go to church also report having a better sex life in marriage. People who take their spirituality seriously are people who pray, and prayer can help you lower your stress by taking time apart from the world to focus on God and not on all the thousands of things you have to do that day. The members of the denomination to which I have the honor of belonging, the Seventh-day Adventist Church, live up to seven years longer than the general population.

3. *Values.* The church teaches biblical values like love, acceptance, forgiveness, repentance, and connection with others who are not like you. Those are all positive personal values that I want my children to have. One of my greatest satisfactions is to see my children make

We All Have ~~Problems~~ Solutions

positive choices based on the principles they were taught at church. The world is a better place when we follow the principles of the Master rather than seeking an eye for an eye. If it's an eye for an eye, the whole world will end up blind. In a world where violence and hate are ever more prevalent, the church has helped me experience peace and learn how to be a peacemaker.

4. *Hope.* There are two ways of looking at life. One is viewing life without God at the center, and the other is viewing life with Him as the Divine Architect. Both outlooks have suffering. People with both outlooks die of cancer and lose their jobs and families. Only one outlook, however, provides hope. I cannot conceive of a life where I am born, I live a life of suffering, I die—and that's it. The church helps me make sense of what happens, even when I don't understand it. It helps me to see things from a perspective of hope and not wave my white flag or take my own life when suffering comes my way. Living with hope makes all the difference.

5. *Conversion.* The church points us to Christ, and Christ converts us. What is conversion? It is the experience in which God takes a person who is living a self-destructive life and gives them the power and grace to experience a change that only He can provide. People

The Problem of Disconnection

who go to church usually have a healthier lifestyle. They eat better. They don't abuse drugs and alcohol, or if they do fall in this area, they understand that such a lifestyle is not God's plan. A converted person is a person who forgives and doesn't hold grudges and therefore lives a happier life. Once again—holding a grudge is like drinking poison and waiting for the rat to die. The church teaches us to live full lives.

I hope that I have at least put in your mind some new ideas outside of the ones you may have had about the church. Think about them. Take a moment to analyze the direction your life, and the life of each family member as well, is taking. Don't judge God by what you see in people at church. Those people, like you, are broken sinners who also need God. I recommend you consider the following:

- The head goes with the body; you can't have one without the other. Saying that you're cool with God but don't want to know anything about church is an impossibility. The Bible itself, inspired by the same God who gave instructions to Moses thousands of years ago, says that He is the Head of the church. You cannot separate the Head from the body, which is the

church. I would not go to my future in-laws' home and say I want to marry their daughter, but I only want to take her head, and they can keep her body. The head and body go together.
- Look for a healthy church. Not every restaurant is clean. If you eat at one restaurant and later you have diarrhea, you don't say, "Well! All restaurants are bad. I am never going to eat out again!" No. You find a different restaurant. Eating out is enjoyable. Find a healthy church. If you need more information, email me at rhvidaministries@gmail.com, and I can send you the name of a church in your city. We created www.helphopehere.com for this reason—so you can find a church with beliefs that are based on what the Bible teaches.
- God is not people, and people are not God. Christians want to be like Christ, but Christ is not like Christians. Christ is perfect, but Christians are not. Christ will never fail you; it could be that a Christian may fail you one day. Do not judge Christ by His followers. Get to know Him. He wants to have a one-on-one relationship with you, and He wants to help you live the life that He dreamed for you.

The Problem of Disconnection

Just as Moses and the Israelites found a much deeper communion with God in the desert, you also can find fresh water for your problems in the church. I'll be waiting for you this coming Sabbath. "And this is the way to have eternal life—to know you, the only true God, and Jesus Christ, the one you sent to earth" (John 17:3).

---

1. T. M. Luhrmann, "The Benefits of Church" *The New York Times*, April 20, 2013, https://www.nytimes.com/2013/04/21/opinion/sunday/luhrmann-why-going-to-church-is-good-for-you.html.

Part 2

We All Have Hope

Lesson 1

Trouble

We All Have Problems—HOPE

Hear

Someone has said that "peace is not the absence of trouble, but the presence of God." In today's lesson we will learn how to act and react when trouble arises. The reality of both problems and blessings is that they often come unannounced. Let's search together for solutions.

Open

1. What two characteristics define our human existence, according to Job?
   - "How frail is humanity! How short is life, how full of trouble!" (Job 14:1).
   - Life is _____.
   - Life is full of _____.

2. The Bible mentions several areas where we may be experiencing trouble. What are they?
   - Trouble in relationships because of lack

We All Have ~~Problems~~ Solutions

or need of money. Read Proverbs 19:4, 7.
- Trouble because of other people's attacks. Read Psalm 25:19.
- Trouble because of our own poor choices or sins. Read Psalm 38:18.

Of these three causes of trouble, which one would you say is presently affecting you?

_____

3. Instead of spending your life concentrating on worrying about your problems, what better option does Scripture suggest we take? Read Philippians 4:6.

_____

4. Paul had his share of difficult situations. Even though he was troubled by his circumstances, what did he experience in the midst of his pain? Read 2 Corinthians 7:4.

_____

5. Read Romans 8:35–37. List at least four things that the Bible guarantees cannot separate you from God and His love.

_____
_____
_____
_____

Trouble

Practice

If and when you experience trouble, remember to apply the following principles to your life:

1. *Pray about it.* "I pour out before him my complaint; before him I tell my trouble" (Psalm 142:2, NIV). You don't have to carry your burden alone. You don't need to feel as though you are fighting by yourself. What problem can you pray for right now? You can write it here if you wish:

   God, please help me with _____.

2. *Don't worry about it.* "Therefore do not worry about tomorrow, for tomorrow will worry about itself. Each day has enough trouble of its own" (Matthew 6:34, NIV). Why? Let me give you three reasons:
   - Worry doesn't make sense. If you can fix it, do it. If you can't, worrying won't make a difference.
   - Worry doesn't make it better. Worry makes it bigger.
   - Worry doesn't increase your faith. By worrying, you minimize God's power and increase your anxiety level.

3. *Trust God to help you through it.* God uses a three-pronged method to deal with our troubles:

We All Have ~~Problems~~ Solutions

   a. He delivers us *from* trouble. "Then they cried out to the Lord in their trouble, and he delivered them from their distress" (Psalm 107:6, NIV).
   b. He comforts us *in* trouble. "[He] comforts us in all our troubles, so that we can comfort those in any trouble with the comfort we ourselves receive from God" (2 Corinthians 1:4, NIV).
   c. He will eventually eliminate *all* trouble. "[He will] give relief to you who are troubled, and to us as well. This will happen when the Lord Jesus is revealed from heaven in blazing fire with his powerful angels" (2 Thessalonians 1:7, NIV).

Empower

My decision today

With God's help, I will seek to worry less, pray more, and trust completely. I will make my requests known to God and will wait on His response. The good news is that God is bigger than any of my problems and that He cares for me.

Lesson 2

Connection

We All Have Problems—HOPE

Hear

Kids' prayers are the best. Before we go on to our study, let's read a short one that will put a smile on your face.

A little boy prayed, "Dear God, please take care of my daddy and my mommy and my sister and my brother and my doggy and me. Oh, please take care of Yourself, God. If anything happens to You, we're gonna be in a big mess."

Open

1. What important thing did the disciples ask Jesus to teach them? Read Luke 11:1.

   _____

2. The Lord's Prayer is a classic prayer, which is found in Matthew 6:9–13. Read it now. What are the first two words?

We All Have ~~Problems~~ Solutions

_____. Why do you think God wants us to see him as a Father? Is it easy or difficult to picture God as a Father? Why?

_____

3. Let's look together at four characteristics of effective prayer:

    a. Prayer is best when it's honest. Read 1 Samuel 1:10.
    b. Prayer admits our weaknesses and protects us in temptation. Read Matthew 26:41.
    c. Prayer works best when it's accompanied with actions. Read 2 Chronicles 7:14.
    d. Prayer is more powerful when we seek God, not just what He can do for us. Read Psalm 66:20.

4. What hinders the effectiveness of prayer? Read Mark 11:25.

    _____
    _____
    _____

5. It is important to ask God for what we need. What else should we do as we pray? Read Philippians 4:6.

    _____
    _____

Connection

Practice

Now comes the time for practice. You may choose to do these prayers now or later by yourself. We can learn these principles together.

God encourages us to do the following:

1. *Be balanced.* Prayer that is effective looks in three directions:

   a. Prayer looks *up*. We focus on God and what He is. When we focus on God, our perspective changes.
   - Read 2 Corinthians 9:8. God is

     _____.

   - Read 1 John 5:14. God is_____.
   - Read Deuteronomy 4:31. God is

     _____.

   b. Prayer looks *inward*. We recognize, confess, and address our sins and shortcomings. Read Psalm 38:18.

   c. Prayer looks *around*. We seek to bless others and pray on their behalf. Read James 5:15.

2. *Be careful.* One of the most important principles that you will learn today is that prayer is seeking God, not just for what He can do for you. He is not a means to an end, even though He is our Provider. When you pray, seek *Him,* not just His blessings.

We All Have ~~Problems~~ Solutions

3. *Be bold.* Read Hebrews 4:16. This passage tells us that, as God's children, we can go to Him without fear. Don't say no to yourself by failing to ask God. Pray according to His will and in Jesus' name, and let Him decide what is best for you.

Empower
My decision today

This week I commit to pray. I will use the three-pronged approach to prayer: I will look up and focus on God first. Then, I will look at myself honestly and address what needs to change within. And finally, as a grateful response to His grace, I will pray and help others. I understand that God accepts and hears my prayer not because of *who* prays, but because He loves to *have* me pray. As I decide to develop my relationship with God through prayer, I understand that the good news is that God hears me and loves to talk to me no matter what I have done or who I am.

Lesson 3

Priorities

We All Have Problems—HOPE

Hear
Start by reading Luke 10:38–42.

Open
1. Who showed up at Martha's house? Read Luke 10:38. (Clue: It's more than one person.)

   _____
   _____

2. Describe Martha's emotions. Write at least three of them here.

   _____
   _____

3. The name Martha means "is becoming bitter." Why do you think Jesus mentions her name twice? What could be making her bitter?

   _____
   _____

We All Have ~~Problems~~ Solutions

4. As you look at Martha's attitude, how do you imagine her talking to Jesus in verse 40?

   _____
   _____

5. Jesus told Martha that Mary had "chosen" what was better. How hard is it for you to take time out of your day to spend with Jesus?

   _____
   _____

Practice

In order to refocus your life, you must make the following three decisions daily:

1. *Choose the important over the urgent.* Mary chose the *important*, while Martha chose the *urgent*. Beware of the "tyranny of the urgent," which seeks to divert you from concentrating on the important issues in life, like God, family, and personal growth. What are one or two urgent things you keep doing that keep you away from the important ones?

   _____
   _____

2. *Choose the best over the good.* The most difficult decision for a Christian is not the choice between good and bad—it's between good

and better. In what areas of your life are you settling for *good enough*?

_____

_____

3. *Choose the permanent over the temporary.* The latest fad—summer blockbusters, phones, clothing—looks to gain our immediate attention. They all have something in common: They are temporary. Don't concentrate your efforts on people, pastimes, and problems that will not be here ten years from now. What is one problem you are fretting about that you know will soon pass?

_____

_____

Empower
My decision today

This week I'll memorize these three words: *important, best, permanent.* Every time a decision needs to be made, I'll ask myself if the choice I'm making is in line with those three words. I will share what I learned this week with a friend who needs to hear it.

Remember, you are not a human *doing*. You are a human *being*. Your actions don't make you more valuable to God. The cross reminds you that Jesus died before you could do something to deserve it.

The gospel says it's done. It's finished. It's complete. Now rest in it.

Lesson 4

Dollars and Sense

We All Have Problems—HOPE

Hear

Money is neither moral nor immoral, neither good nor bad. It's like a brick that can either be used to build a nice chimney or break the window of the neighbor who plays loud music at 3 A.M. The problem is not money itself, but how it's used. It adopts the characteristics of its owner and makes that person more of what he or she already is.

Open

1. "Suppose one of you wants to *build* a tower. Won't you first *sit down* and estimate the cost to see if you *have enough* money to *complete it*?" (Luke 14:28, NIV; emphasis added). This short verse has four biblical principles for better administration of our finances. Answer the questions that follow the principles.

   a. *Set goals.* The goal of the man was

Dollars and Sense

to build a tower. What are your financial goals? Write one down here:

_____

b. *Think first.* What did the man do before he began to build? Are you an impulse buyer, or do you think first?

_____
_____

c. *Budget expenses.* What is the true purpose of a budget? What holds you back from developing one for yourself?
d. *Always persevere.* Is it easy or difficult for you to finish what you begin?

2. The book of Job has a great passage concerning finances. It reads: "If they obey and serve him, they will spend the rest of their days in prosperity and their years in contentment" (Job 36:11, NIV). According to this verse, what is our role regarding finances? We should obey and _____ God.
3. Jesus told a sobering story of the ever-present danger of concentrating too much on material items. Read Luke 12:16–21. What lesson do you think Jesus was trying to teach us?

_____

4. One of the most freeing aspects of the gospel (good news) is that our worth is

We All Have ~~Problems~~ Solutions

not in what we produce, gain, or possess. Instead, what does Jesus invites us to freely receive? Read Revelation 22:17.

_____

Practice

Here are three more practical lessons about finances:

1. *Don't let yourself be enticed.* The Bible gives the following advice in Job 36:18: "Be careful that no one entices you by riches" (NIV). Is there an object in your life that is enticing you to fall in love with it?

   _____

2. *Don't become obsessed.* Check all that apply to you (these will not be discussed out loud, they're personal).
   - ❏ Do you neglect your family because of your work?
   - ❏ Is it hard for you to leave your work behind at your worksite?
   - ❏ Do you continue thinking about work during vacations and times of rest?
   - ❏ Do you think about work first thing when you get up and last thing as you go to sleep?
   - ❏ Do you think about work or your finances when you pray, read the Bible, or are in church?

Dollars and Sense

- ❑ In selecting your career, were you thinking about how much money you would earn?
- ❑ Do you buy things on sale even though you don't need them?
- ❑ When you go out to eat, do you eat more when someone else is paying?
- ❑ Is making money the object of your life?

3. *Don't commit yourself to others' debts.* The Bible is clear about this. Proverbs 22:26, 27 counsels us, "Don't promise to be responsible for someone else's debts. If you should be unable to pay, they will take away even your bed" (GNT). What danger does a person face who signs for another's debt? Mention two reasons it's not advisable to do so.

_____
_____

Empower

When the famous magnate John D. Rockefeller died, someone asked his bookkeeper, "How much money did Rockefeller leave?"

The bookkeeper replied, "He left everything."

My decision today

With God's help, I choose to manage my finances in a way that honors God and values my health and my family. I pray to find my worth in what God accomplished for me on the cross and not in my temporary earthly accomplishments.

The gospel frees you from having to produce in order to be noticed, loved, or valued. You are valued, loved, and accepted because of His sacrifice, not your success.

You are loved. Period.

Lesson 5

Hurt

We All Have Problems—HOPE

Hear
"I hurt with the hurt of my people. I mourn and am overcome with grief. Is there no medicine in Gilead? Is there no physician there? Why is there no healing for the wounds of my people" (Jeremiah 8:21, 22).

Everyone has experienced hurt. For some, emotional and physical pain are constant reminders that words and actions matter. Once again, this is a topic that Scripture addresses at length.

Open
There are several causes of pain. Among them are physical, spiritual, mental/emotional, and sexual abuse. We usually fall into one of two categories: We have either experienced abuse, or we know a person who has.

1. Who is responsible for the pain in this world? Read Revelation 12:9.

We All Have ~~Problems~~ Solutions

2. There are at least four reasons for your pain. Take a moment to look at the four categories below, then analyze your painful experiences and ascribe a percentage to each one:

- Intentional hurt from others _____
- Unintentional hurt from others _____
- Intentional hurt from yourself _____
- Unintentional hurt from yourself _____

3. Even in Bible times, God provided guidelines for respect and consequences for abuse of every kind. Let's review two of them:

    a. *Abuse through incest.* Read Deuteronomy 27:22.
    b. *Respect for and care of children.* Read Matthew 18:6.

4. Hurt can create deep wounds, especially if you don't talk about it and forgive it. Hurt prospers in secrecy. Here are two suggestions from the Bible about the importance of sharing your struggles:

    a. How did David feel when he wasn't able to speak about his situation? Read Psalm 32:3. Why is it important to share with a responsible and qualified person what happened to us?

b. What is another blessing of sharing your pain with another? Read James 5:16.

_____

5. Why is it so important to forgive? What does forgiving really mean? What is one thing we can do? Read Luke 6:28.

_____

6. What can we do for people who have experienced hurt? Read Hebrews 12:12, 13; Isaiah 35:3, 4.

_____

7. What does God promise concerning the end of all hurt? Revelation 21:3, 4.

_____

Practice

These are three important actions you can take:

1. *Deal with it correctly.* According to recent findings, more than half of women and at least forty percent of men experience abuse. How do we deal with it? Some try to bury it, ignore it, or mitigate the pain with addiction. Instead, speak about it, address it, and understand how God can bring healing to your life. What proactive steps are you taking to address the pain in your life?
2. *Forgive it completely.* Holding in resentment

is like drinking rat poison and hoping the rat will die. Therefore, you must forgive. Forgiving does not mean the restoration of the relationship or welcoming into your home a known abuser. It means that you treat with respect and love the one who hurt you. If you have been a victim, the first step is to forgive. Whom do you need to forgive today?
3. *Grow from it immediately.* The moment you forgive, you start growing. As you leave the past behind, sharing your experiences can help other people, either by keeping them from suffering what you did or by comforting those who can identify with your pain.

Empower
My decision today
This week pray for God to help you do the following three things: deal with, forgive, and grow from painful experiences in your life. If you have never had such things happen to you, be thankful and look for ways to bless others who have.

The cross of Christ shows us that the God of the Bible saw our plight, entered our suffering, endured our trials, and can restore all things. While other religions teach that man can work himself upward to get to God, Christianity shows a God who descends and rescues us. He seldom provides answers; He ultimately provides solutions.

Lesson 6

Transformation

We All Have Problems—HOPE

Hear
We were created for relationships. They determine in large part our well-being. Billy Graham had it right when he stated, "God is more interested in your future and your relationships than you are." But life is painful. That's why Jesus has promised to return to complete our transformation. His second coming is good news.

Open
Revelation 21:4 says, "He will wipe every tear from their eyes, and there will be no more death or sorrow or crying or pain. All these things are gone forever."

Isaiah 65:17 says, "Look! I am creating new heavens and a new earth."

1. How did God want people to live? Read Genesis 1:26.

We All Have ~~Problems~~ Solutions

2. What interfered with the plans God had for His children? Read Genesis 3:1–13.

   _____

3. What did God do to transform the situation? Read John 3:16.

   _____

4. At what point does our transformation begin? Read 2 Corinthians 5:17.

   _____

5. God promises to transform our reality permanently when He comes back. What four things does God promise to eliminate forever? Read Revelation 21:4.

   a. _____
   b. _____
   c. _____
   d. _____

Practice

The way in which God transforms the human being occurs in three stages:

1. *When we accept the sacrifice of Jesus, the transformation begins.* We must invite Him to live in our lives and begin a daily relationship with Him. We are transformed into new creatures. This is known as a spiritual new birth,

Transformation

or conversion. Have you invited Jesus to be your Savior?

2. *As we walk with Christ, the transformation continues.* Throughout the Christian life, spiritual transformation occurs, and we begin to see spiritual fruit, such as patience, kindness, self-control, and joy. The purpose of this process is that every day we look more like Jesus. This stage is called sanctification.
3. *When Jesus Christ comes the second time, He will complete the transformation.* Christ promised to return to transform the reality of humanity forever.

The Bible tells us, "Then I saw a new heaven and a new earth, for the old heaven and the old earth had disappeared. And the sea was also gone" (Revelation 21:1). Isaiah 65:17 confirms this when it says, "I am creating new heavens and a new earth, and no one will even think about the old ones anymore."

Identify the things you want God to transform in your life permanently as you prepare for His second coming:

- ❑ Relationships
- ❑ Character
- ❑ Finance
- ❑ Work
- ❑ Decision-making
- ❑ Other: _____

Identify areas of your life in which you have not yet permitted God to transform you (family, work, finances, marriage, character, grudges, wounds, etc).

_____
_____

Recognize the promise of God to transform your life forever, and memorize Revelation 21:4: "He will wipe every tear from [my eyes], and there will be no more death or sorrow or crying or pain. All these things are gone forever."

Empower
My decision today

I will intentionally seek to surround myself with people who will build me up and not tear me down, people who are interested in my transformation. I will put my trust in Jesus and find my acceptance first and foremost from my Father, who promised to come back for me and finish my transformation. Since the gospel frees me from fear, I realize that I am loved and accepted by God because of His son Jesus, who is not only my Savior, but also my Friend. He loves me, warts and all, and will soon return for me.

Lesson 7

Failure

We All Have Problems—HOPE

Hear
Vince Lombardi once said, "If it doesn't matter who wins or loses, then why do they keep score?"

We all like winners. That's why we keep score. If truthful, we will admit that there are areas in our lives in which we could be doing better.

Right off the bat, let's remember three powerful principles as we deal with this topic:

- Failure is an event, not an identity.
- You can fail, but you are not a failure.
- Everyone fails—everyone. It's a matter of when, not if.

Open
1. Why do people fail? "Pride leads to destruction, and arrogance to downfall" (Proverbs 16:18, GNT). The main reason is that we are_____ and _____.

We All Have ~~Problems~~ Solutions

The three most dangerous words in the English language are "I already know!" "Good planning and hard work lead to prosperity, but hasty *shortcuts* lead to poverty" (Proverbs 21:5; emphasis added). We fail because we take _____. In what areas do you tend to take shortcuts? Feel free to either share or just reflect privately. Mark all that apply:

- ❏ Relationships
- ❏ Exercise/diet
- ❏ Finances
- ❏ Education
- ❏ Spirituality
- ❏ Other _____

2. When we fail, it's important to examine ourselves and find out why it happened. After we have taken an honest look at ourselves, what is a great step to take? Read Lamentations 3:40, and write your thoughts here.

_____
_____
_____

3. An important step to take when you fail is to look in Scripture for hope, claiming the promises of God for your life. Read these three beautiful promises that you can

Failure

apply today: Psalm 50:15; Psalm 34:7; and Isaiah 41:10.

Practice

Different people will have different reactions when they fail. Here are three common ones:

1. *Some will quit.* "If your boss is angry at you, don't quit! A quiet spirit can overcome even great mistakes" (Ecclesiastes 10:4). Don't give up on God. Don't give up on relationships. Don't give up on your dreams.
2. *Some will blame.* "Then Sarai said to Abram, 'This is all your fault! I put my servant into your arms, but now that she's pregnant she treats me with contempt. The LORD will show who's wrong—you or me!' " (Genesis 16:5).
3. *Some will grow.* "I have not yet reached my goal, and I am not perfect. But Christ has taken hold of me. So I *keep on* running and struggling to take hold of the prize. My friends, I don't feel that I have already arrived. But I forget what is behind, and I struggle for what is ahead. I run toward the goal, so that I can win the prize of being called to heaven. This is the prize that God offers because of what Christ Jesus has done" (Philippians 3:12–14, CEV; emphasis added).

Empower

My decision today

With God's help, I will remember that failure is an event, not an identity. I can learn from my failures, but I won't be defined by them. Christ's death and resurrection teach me that, from my darkest hour, great blessings can come. I choose to trust Jesus and His plan instead of my own.

Lesson 8

Rest

We All Have Problems—HOPE

Hear
It's been dubbed the twenty-first-century equivalent of the Black Death. In the UK, it's the most common reason employees take long-term sick leave. It costs American companies three hundred billion dollars a year. In Japan, it's a fatal epidemic. What is it? Stress. Let's look at the antidote. "The LORD replied, 'My Presence will go with you, and I will give you rest' " (Exodus 33:14, NIV).

Open
We have two important decisions regarding rest, balance, and the Sabbath:

    A. *Choose the important over the urgent.* Because God knew that we would struggle with balance, He gave us the Sabbath.
    B. *Choose better over good.* Some have said you can worship God on any day of the week.

We All Have ~~Problems~~ Solutions

> While this is partially true, it is scripturally sound to set apart the seventh day as a day of rest and intentional worship.

1. What three things did God Himself do on the Sabbath? _____, _____, and _____.
"Thus the heavens and the earth were completed in all their vast array. By the seventh day God had finished the work he had been doing; so on the seventh day he rested from all his work. Then God blessed the seventh day and made it holy, because on it he rested from all the work of creating that he had done" (Genesis 2:1–3, NIV).

2. How is the Sabbath called in Scripture? It is a _____. "They must realize that the Sabbath is the LORD's gift to you. That is why he gives you a two-day supply on the sixth day, so there will be enough for two days. On the Sabbath day you must each stay in your place. Do not go out to pick up food on the seventh day" (Exodus 16:29).

3. Don't settle for good when better is available. Note the best in the texts below:
   - In Genesis, God rested, called it holy and blessed it (Genesis 2:1–3).
   - In Exodus, Sabbath is the fourth com-

Rest

mandment (Exodus 20:8–11).
- Jesus worshiped on the seventh day, "as was his custom" (Luke 4:16, NIV).
- Mary rested on the Sabbath (Luke 23:56).
- The disciples worshiped after the resurrection (Acts 13:42).
- Paul worshiped on the Sabbath (Acts 17:2).
- In the new earth, the tradition continues (Isaiah 66:22, 23).

Practice

1. What blessings can you point out as a result of keeping the Sabbath?
    a. "Keep the Sabbath day holy. Don't pursue your own interests on that day, but enjoy the Sabbath and speak of it with delight as the Lord's holy day. Honor the Sabbath in everything you do on that day, and don't follow your own desires or talk idly. Then the Lord will be your delight. I will give you great honor and satisfy you with the inheritance I promised to your ancestor Jacob. I, the Lord, have spoken!" (Isaiah 58:13, 14).
2. The Sabbath is a gift of rest in two main ways:
    a. *It's grace-oriented.* "You have six days each week for your ordinary work, but the seventh day is a Sabbath day of rest

We All Have ~~Problems~~ Solutions

dedicated to the Lord your God. On that day no one in your household may do any work. This includes you, your sons and daughters, your male and female servants, your oxen and donkeys and other livestock, and any foreigners living among you. All your male and female servants must rest as you do. Remember that you were once slaves in Egypt, but the Lord your God brought you out with his strong hand and powerful arm. That is why the Lord your God has commanded you to rest on the Sabbath day" (Deuteronomy 5:13–15).
b. *It's permanent.* "All your words are true; all your righteous laws are eternal" (Psalm 119:160, NIV).

Empower
My decision today

I accept that, on my own, it will be very difficult to achieve balance. I receive the gift of the Sabbath and thank God for his sacrifice for me, and by the grace of God, I seek to rest, delight, and worship on this day, as God requires.

Lesson 9

Life

We All Have Problems—HOPE

Hear

After church, where she had been taught about the Second Coming, a little girl quizzed her mother. "Mommy, do you believe Jesus will come back?"

"Yes."

"Today?"

"Yes."

"In a few minutes?"

"Yes, dear."

"Mommy, would you comb my hair?"

Open

"Brothers and sisters, we do not want you to be uninformed about those who sleep in death, so that you do not grieve like the rest of mankind, who have no hope. For we believe that *Jesus died and rose again*, and so we believe that God will bring with Jesus those who have fallen asleep in him. According to the Lord's own word, we tell you that we who are still alive, who are left until the coming of the Lord, *will certainly not precede* those who have fallen asleep. *For the Lord himself will come down from heaven,* with a loud command, with the voice of the archangel and with the trumpet call of God, and *the dead in Christ will rise first.* After that, we who are still alive and are left will be caught up *together* with them in the clouds to meet the Lord in the air. And so we will be with the Lord forever. Therefore encourage one another with these words" (1 Thessalonians 4:13–18, NIV; emphasis added).

As you read the text above, answer these questions:

1. Will the dead precede the living to heaven?

   _____

2. When will the resurrection happen?

   _____

3. Who will call the dead to life?

   _____

4. Who will rise first?

   _____

5. What guarantees our resurrection (verse 14)?

   _____

Life

Practice

1. *Believe in the risen Savior.* The most awesome thing about death is that Jesus already defeated it! He even mocks it (1 Corinthians 15)! But the good news is that He wants to share that victory with us. He created us to live, and as we connect with Him, the Source of life, we have life. Have you surrendered your life to Jesus? Trust your life to Him today. Whom have you lost that you would like to see again?

   _____

2. *Understand death.* People have many different ideas about what happens when we die. The Bible is not silent on this subject. Here are some facts: Life equals God's breath + body (Genesis 2:7). Death is the reverse (Ecclesiastes 12:7). When we die, we are dead (Ecclesiastes 9:5, 6; Psalm 104:29; Psalm 146:4; Acts 2:29, 34). The word "soul" is a widely misunderstood concept. It means a "living being," which the Bible says will die (Ezekiel 18:4, 20). People who die are neither in heaven nor in hell. They are asleep. Those who die having accepted Jesus as their Lord and Savior are waiting to hear the powerful voice of their Creator. What are some of the misconceptions in movies and TV shows about what happens when we die?

   _____

3. *Wait for the Second Coming.* Luke 14:14 says that we will enjoy heaven at the second coming of Jesus, not before. Jesus comes to reward all of us, according to what we have done—but none go ahead of the rest (Revelation 22:12). We will all go together. We will enter heaven and receive life *together*. It will be a great reunion.

Empower
My decision today

Do you want to be there? Then make the best decision ever: Give your life to Jesus today. Live life as if He will come today. Have you lost a loved one—maybe a friend, a family member, or spouse? Are you concerned about your own future? This week find hope in the promise of the resurrection of Jesus.

Lesson 10

Faith

We All Have Problems—HOPE

Hear

There are four questions that people like us have asked themselves throughout history:

1. Where do I come from?
2. How should I live?
3. What is the purpose of my life?
4. Where am I going?

The gospel (good news) answers these questions. The gospel *is* good news, not just good advice. What's the good news? Let's study the basic tenets of the gospel according to Jesus.

Open

There are five significant components of the gospel:

1. *What we are.* How does the Bible describe the human condition? Read Romans 3:10–12.

We All Have ~~Problems~~ Solutions

We are _____. Read
Ephesians 2:1. We are _____.

2. *Accountability for our actions.* Every action and decision has a consequence. Read Hebrews 9:27. Think about it. Accountability is built into us. We demand it from our civic leaders, teachers, and family. In a macro sense, God will hold us accountable for the decisions we have made.
3. *The inability to make it right on our own.* Enter Jesus. What did Jesus do about our condition? Read Colossians 2:13.

   _____

4. *The death and resurrection of Jesus is a historical fact we can accept or deny.* Read 1 Corinthians 15:1–8. Take the time to analyze the details in that passage.
5. *Our acceptance of the gospel results in life transformation.* Notice this passage: "[For]our gospel came to you not simply with words but with power, with the Holy Spirit and deep conviction" (1 Thessalonians 1:5, NIV).

A changed life is not the means to salvation, but it is definitely the result of understanding and experiencing the gospel in your life.

Practice

Here is the best summary concerning the gospel:

Faith

1. *A relationship with Jesus affects our past.*
   Read 2 Corinthians 5:17. We have all made mistakes, errors, and wrong choices that have produced pain in ourselves and others. The process of dealing with the past starts with two elements:

   a. *Confession.* When you confess your sins to God, you admit responsibility.
   b. *Repentance.* When you repent, you recognize that change is needed.

2. *A relationship with Jesus affects our present.*
   Living as a person who has been forgiven has practical implications. Notice this passage: "Put all your rebellion behind you, and find yourselves a new heart and a new spirit. For why should you die, O people of Israel?" (Ezekiel 18:31). It's freeing to know we don't have to live shackled by past mistakes and worried about future issues. Because we have been forgiven and accepted by God, we can do the same for others.

3. *A relationship with God affects our future.*
   Read Psalm 31:15. One of the most important ways the gospel affects our lives is in helping us live with the hope of a better future. All through Scripture, prophecies are made about deliverance, salvation, and restoration. We can know our future is secure

when we see how God has fulfilled His prophecies in the past.

Empower

My decision today

I acknowledge that I am a sinner. I give control of my life to God and ask Jesus to be my Savior and Leader. I believe that no matter how awful my sins, God is not mad at me. Instead, my heavenly Father allowed Jesus to take upon Himself all the guilt, shame, and rejection I deserve. I choose to follow Christ.

Discover Online

FREE Lessons at www.BibleStudies.com

Call:
1-888-456-7933

Write:
Discover
P.O. Box 999
Loveland, CO 80539-0999

It's easy to learn more about the Bible!